PLAY & LEARN
WITH RUBBER STAMPS

Compiled by Elizabeth McKinnon
Illustrated by Gary Mohrmann

Warren Publishing House, Inc.
Everett, Washington

We wish to acknowledge the following teachers, parents, and child-care workers who contributed ideas to this book: Gillian Adams, Newark, NJ; Ellen Bedford, Bridgeport, CT; Jamie Bedford, Bridgeport, CT; Scott Bedford, Bridgeport, CT; Karen Blaser, Alliance, OH; Janice Bodenstedt, Jackson, MI; Susan Burbridge, Albuquerque, NM; Diane Cherry, Delray Beach, FL; Tamara Clohessy, Eureka, CA; Marcia Dedenbach, Hawthorne, FL; Ruth Engle, Kirkland, WA; Rita Galloway, Harlingen, TX; Connie Gillilan, Hardy, NE; Kaline A. Goodrich, Bangor, ME; Angela Hannaford, Rancho Murieta, CA; Shelley Hansen, Wichita, KS; Janetlynne Hood, Longs, SC; Joan Hunter, Elbridge, NY; Martha Magnia, Fresno, CA; Kathy McCullough, Everett, WA; Richard McKinnon, Seattle, WA; Susan A. Miller, Kutztown, PA; Ann M. O'Connell, Coaldale, PA; Sharon Olson, Minot, ND; Lillian Osborne, St. Charles, MI; Susan Peters, Upland, CA; Beverly Qualheim, Marquette, MI; Christine Robertson, Oakmont, PA; Debbie Rowley, Redmond, WA; Kathy Sizer, Tustin, CA; Jackie Smallwood, Royersford, PA; Diane Thom, Maple Valley, WA; Gail A. Weidner, Tustin, CA; Marie Wheeler, Tacoma, WA; Kathy Wolfe, Chagrin Falls, OH; Mary Zorn, Fort Morgan, CO; Deborah Zumbar, Alliance, OH.

EDITORIAL STAFF:

Editorial Manager: Kathleen Cubley
Editors: Gayle Bittinger, Susan Hodges, Jean Warren
Copy Editor: Miriam Bulmer
Proofreader: Mae Rhodes
Editorial Assistant: Erica West

DESIGN AND PRODUCTION STAFF:

Art Manager: Jill Lustig
Book Design/Layout: Lynne Faulk, Sarah Ness
Cover Design: Brenda Mann Harrison, Mae Rhodes
Cover Illustration: Kathy Kotomaimoce
Production Manager: Jo Anna Brock

ISBN 0-911019-93-6

Library of Congress Catalog Number 93-61083
Printed in the United States of America
Published by: Warren Publishing House, Inc.
          P.O. Box 2250
          Everett, WA 98203

20 19 18 17 16 15 14 13 12 11 10 9 8 7 6 5 4 3 2 1

INTRODUCTION

Young children love playing with rubber stamps. This book is designed to help you turn that play into learning opportunities.

Rubber stamps are so versatile, you'll be amazed at the ideas your children come up with for using them. And with all the different types of activities offered in *Play and Learn With Rubber Stamps*, the possibilities are endless. You'll find that simple stamps are just as popular with your children as fancy stamps, and that an old lunch sack is just as much fun to stamp on as a new sheet of paper.

As you look through the book, you will find open-ended activity suggestions for art, language, learning games, math, science, and music. You will also find ideas for using rubber stamps to make teaching materials, and suggestions for making your own stamps.

We believe that the ideas in this book will prove to be exciting and successful, both for you and for your children. Happy stamping!

CONTENTS

ART

Rubber Stamp Learning Center

Set up a learning center where your children can experiment with using rubber stamps. Include colored washable-ink pads, a variety of rubber stamps, and different kinds of paper such as newsprint, construction paper, tissue paper, brown wrapping paper, and paper from junk mail. Show your children how to ink and print a stamp, moving it straight down and straight up without rocking your hand. Keep the work area covered with fresh paper to use for practice stamping and for blotting stamps clean after use.

NOTE: Rubber stamps and stamping materials are available at places such as school and office supply stores, toy stores, gift shops, and craft stores. For ideas on making your own stamps, see pages 56–61. Unless otherwise indicated, it is recommended that you always use washable inks when doing stamping activities with young children.

Totem Pole Art

Display pictures of totem poles and discuss them with your children. Set out an assortment of animal rubber stamps and different-colored ink pads. Then give your children narrow strips of construction paper and let them stamp on animal designs, one on top of the other, to make their own totem pole pictures. Mount the pictures on colored construction paper and display them on a wall or a bulletin board.

Flower Pictures

Give each of your children a piece of white or light blue construction paper. Set out rubber stamps in the shapes of various flowers. Let the children use the stamps with different-colored ink pads to make flower prints all over their papers. Then have them use green crayons or felt-tip markers to add stems, leaves, and grass.

Farmyard Mural

Use felt-tip markers to draw a simple farmyard scene on a large piece of paper. For example, you might include pictures of a barn, a fence, and a haystack. Place the paper on a low table or on the floor. Provide colored ink pads and rubber stamps in the shapes of farm animals. Have your children ink the stamps and then press them all over the farmyard scene. Display the completed mural on a wall or a bulletin board.

VARIATION: Draw a zoo scene or an underwater scene on a large piece of paper and have your children stamp on pictures of appropriate animals.

Magic Monster Shoes

Find an old pair of child-size tennis shoes. Use a hot glue gun to attach several thin, flat rubber stamps to the soles of the shoes. (Make sure that the stamps are positioned evenly on the shoe soles.) Spread out butcher paper on the floor and pour a small amount of tempera paint into a shallow pan. Let your children take turns putting on the shoes, stepping into the paint, and making "magic monster tracks" all over the butcher paper.

VARIATION: Instead of attaching rubber stamps to the shoe soles, glue on large shapes cut from an inner tube or shoe insoles (see pages 56–57).

Playdough Cookie Designs

Make playdough and give some to each child. Have your children roll out their playdough until it is thin and flat. Let them use cookie cutters to cut out cookie shapes. Then give them dry rubber stamps and have them gently press the stamp designs into their cookies. Encourage the children to use their playdough over again to make new cookie shapes. At the end of the activity, wash and dry the stamps thoroughly before putting them away.

EXTENSION: Use the stamped cookies to make ornaments. Poke a hole in the top of each one for inserting a hanger. Then allow the cookies to air-dry on a flat surface.

Stained Glass

Cover a low table with white butcher paper. Place a sheet of colored cellophane on top of the paper and lightly secure the edges with masking tape. Provide your children with seasonal rubber stamps and colored ink pads. Let them stamp designs all over the cellophane (the butcher paper will allow the stamped designs to be seen clearly). When the ink has dried, remove the cellophane from the table and tape it to a window.

VARIATION: Let your children stamp designs on rectangles of different-colored cellophane. Tape the rectangles to a window to resemble stained glass panes.

Personal Portfolios

Make a portfolio for each of your children by putting two large pieces of construction paper together and stapling around three edges. Set out a variety of rubber stamps and different-colored ink pads. Let your children stamp designs all over their portfolios any way they wish. When they have finished, write each child's name on his or her portfolio. At the end of the day (or week), put the children's artwork and other papers into their portfolios for them to take home.

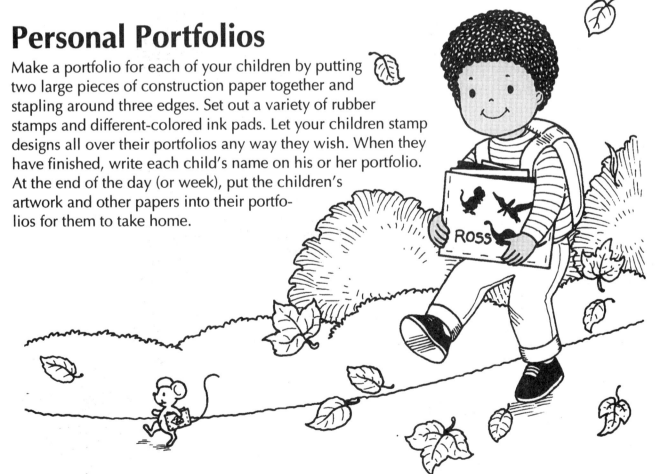

Handmade Wallpaper

Place several pieces of butcher paper on the floor. Set out rubber stamps and two or three different-colored ink pads. Let your children stamp designs on the butcher paper pieces to make wallpaper. Hang the wallpaper in the housekeeping area or use it to line the walls of a cardboard box playhouse.

Gift-Wrap Fun

Choose large paper such as newsprint, butcher paper, tissue paper, or plain wrapping paper. Set out seasonal rubber stamps and ink pads in appropriate colors. Let your children stamp designs all over the paper to create gift wrap. If desired, let them add decorations by coloring with felt-tip markers or gluing on glitter. For coordinated gift wrap, have the children stamp matching designs on paper gift tags.

VARIATION: Instead of using new paper to make gift wrap, let your children stamp colored designs on sheets of black and white newspaper. Or have them decorate the plain sides of large brown grocery bags that have been cut into sheets.

Holiday Ideas

Rubber stamps are always fun to use at holiday times. Following are just a few ideas you might want to try.

Halloween—Set out several jumbo pumpkins and let your children take turns stamping designs on them. Wash off the designs at the end of each day.

Hanukkah—Let your children stamp blue designs on white paper.

Christmas—Have your children print rubber stamp "ornaments" on triangle trees cut from green posterboard.

Chinese New Year—In a library, find a copy of the Chinese zodiac to discover which animal the new year is named for (the mouse, the ox, the tiger, etc.). Let your children use rubber stamps in the shape of that animal to make greeting cards.

Valentine's Day—Give your children white paper lunch sacks. Let them stamp the sacks with red hearts to make valentine bags.

St. Patrick's Day—Have your children print dark green shamrocks on light green paper.

Easter—Let your children use small rubber stamps with bright-colored ink pads to print designs on hard-cooked, dyed Easter eggs.

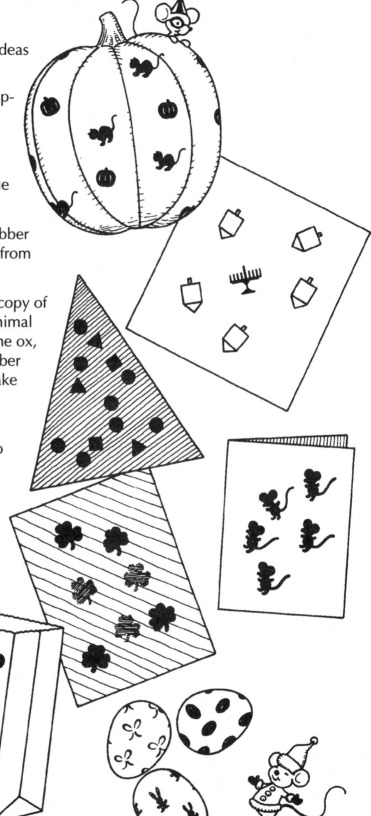

Decorated Picture Mats

For each of your children, purchase a small precut picture mat (available where picture frames are sold). Set out an assortment of small rubber stamps and different-colored ink pads. Let the children decorate their mats by stamping on the designs they wish. Mount pieces of the children's artwork on cardboard and attach them to the backs of their decorated mats so that the pictures show through the openings. Let the children give their matted pictures to relatives or friends as gifts.

Bookmark Gifts

Cut construction paper into 2½-by-7½-inch strips. Set out rubber stamps in seasonal shapes (pumpkins, hearts, eggs, etc.). Also set out ink pads in seasonal colors. Let your children stamp designs on the paper strips to make bookmarks. Help them write their names on the backs. Then cover the bookmarks on both sides with clear self-stick paper. For a finishing touch, punch a hole in the top of each bookmark and tie on a loop of colorful yarn.

Fancy Placemats

Let your children make placemats to use at snack time or to give as gifts. Provide each child with a sheet of light-colored construction paper. Set out the desired shapes of rubber stamps and colored ink pads. Show the children how to stamp borders around the edges of their papers. Then let them decorate the centers of their papers any way they wish. Have the papers laminated or cover them with clear self-stick paper for durability.

Decorated Labels

Give each of your children a strip of six or more self-stick mailing labels (available at office supply stores). Set out rubber stamps and ink pads in light colors. Let your children stamp designs all over their label strips, covering them completely. When the ink has dried, help each child put his or her decorated label strip into an envelope to make a gift for a relative or a friend. The recipient can write over the stamped-on designs before attaching the labels to letters or other items.

Designer T-Shirts

Have each of your children bring in an old, plain T-shirt (or purchase inexpensive T-shirts yourself). Lay the shirts out flat and slip sheets of thin cardboard inside them. Let your children use large rubber stamps with stamp-pad inks sold for use on fabrics to print designs on their T-shirts. (Have the children wear smocks to protect their clothing.) Allow the ink to dry before removing the cardboard inserts.

VARIATION: Instead of fabric inks, use indelible ink pads. Or ink the stamps by coloring them with permanent felt-tip markers. For the best results, test the stamps and inks on T-shirt fabric before doing the activity.

Gift Scratch Pads

Collect unmarked scrap paper you have saved for recycling. Cut the paper into the desired size to make a scratch pad for each child. Staple the pages of each child's pad together. Then have the child use a favorite rubber stamp to decorate a bottom corner of each page. Let the children give their decorated scratch pads as gifts.

Personalized Note Cards

For each of your children, collect several identical note-size envelopes. Cut and fold sheets of light-colored paper to fit inside the envelopes. Set out a variety of small rubber stamps and different-colored ink pads. Let the children decorate the fronts of their folded papers by stamping on designs any way they wish. Or have them just stamp borders across the bottom edges of the papers. Then let the children stamp matching designs or borders on the backs of their envelopes. Tie each child's folded note papers and envelopes together with ribbon to make a gift for a relative or a friend.

Gift Envelope

Provide each of your children with four to six white envelopes. Set out rubber stamps and ink pads in light colors. Have the children stamp designs all over the fronts and outside back flaps of their envelopes. When the ink has dried, tie each child's envelopes together with ribbon to make a gift pack to take home. The recipients can address the envelopes right over the stamped-on designs.

Bulletin Board Borders

On a table or on the floor, lay out long strips of adding machine tape (available at office supply stores). Set out one or two rubber stamps in seasonal shapes, such as pumpkins or hearts, along with ink pads in appropriate colors. Let your children ink the stamps and print lines of designs along the strips of adding machine tape. Use the strips to make borders for your seasonal bulletin boards.

Recycled Border

Instead of buying a new border when you are changing a bulletin board display, try this. Turn over pieces of an old border and spread them out on a low table or on the floor. Give your children rubber stamps that are appropriate for your new display (leaf stamps for an autumn bulletin board, fish stamps for an under-sea bulletin board, etc.). Let the children decorate the back sides of the old border pieces with stamped designs to make a new, one-of-a-kind border.

Bulletin Board Backgrounds

Let your children help make backgrounds for your bulletin board displays. Place butcher paper on the floor, along with colored ink pads and appropriate rubber stamps. For example, set out snowflake stamps for making a winter background, raindrop stamps for making a weather unit background, or flower stamps for making a spring garden background. Have the children stamp the designs all over the butcher paper. When they have finished, attach the paper to a bulletin board and add appropriate bulletin board figures.

VARIATION: If you do not have a bulletin board, hang the decorated butcher paper on a wall and attach paper figures to it with tape.

Picture Frames

Cut frames for your children's artwork out of light-colored construction paper, posterboard, or cardboard. Let your children decorate the frames by printing on designs with rubber stamps. Attach the children's pictures to the backs of the frames and display them around the room.

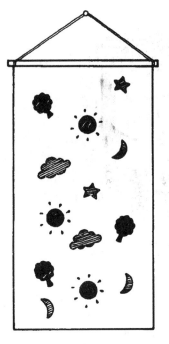
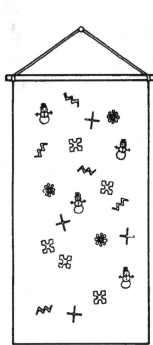

Stamped Banners

Give each of your children a long, narrow piece of light-colored construction paper. Set out rubber stamps and ink pads in various colors. Let the children decorate their papers by stamping on designs any way they wish. Then turn each child's paper into a banner by gluing a short dowel piece to one end and attaching a yarn hanger. Display the finished banners around your room.

VARIATION: For smaller banners, use plastic straws instead of dowel pieces.

Festive Streamers

Set out lengths of light-colored crepe-paper streamers. Give your children rubber stamps in seasonal shapes, such as hearts or shamrocks, along with ink pads in appropriate colors. Let the children decorate the streamer pieces with stamped-on designs. Then hang the streamers around the room for a festive look.

VARIATION: Use strips of adding machine tape instead of crepe-paper streamers.

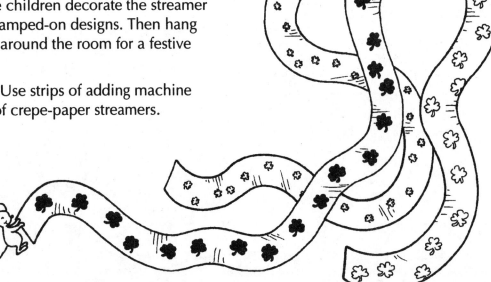

Party Tablecloth

Purchase a plain white paper tablecloth. Cover the work area with butcher paper and place the tablecloth on top of it. Set out large rubber stamps in seasonal or party shapes, along with colored ink pads. Let your children stamp the designs all over the tablecloth to make a festive cover for the snack table. (Keep in mind that spills may cause the inks in the designs to run.)

Decorative Seating Mats

Ask a local pizza restaurant to donate new, large cardboard pizza circles (one for each child). Let your children decorate the circles with rubber stamp designs. Use a permanent marker to write each child's name on his or her decorated circle. Then cover the circles with clear self-stick paper for durability. Keep the decorated circles handy to use for seating mats at group time.

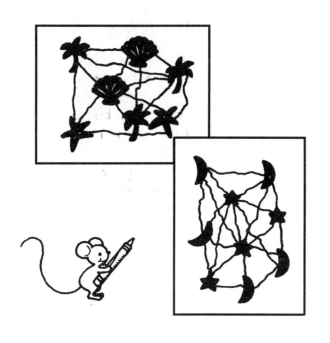

Connecting Designs

Give each of your children a piece of light-colored construction paper. Set out rubber stamps, colored ink pads, and crayons. Let each child use a stamp to print designs at random on his or her paper. Then have the child draw lines with a crayon from one design to the other until all the designs are linked. Display the children's papers on a wall or a bulletin board.

Roller Stamp Fun

Set out colored ink pads and several roller stamps (available where rubber stamps are sold). On a piece of butcher paper, draw long, gently curving lines. Let your children ink the roller stamps and use them to trace over the lines on the butcher paper. If desired, continue adding lines for the children to trace until the entire paper is filled with colorful designs.

VARIATION: Draw giant alphabet letters on butcher paper and have your children trace over them with the inked roller stamps.

Shape Outlines

On a piece of light-colored paper for each child, draw dots to make a large outline of a seasonal shape (a star, a heart, an egg, etc.). Be sure to leave some room between the dots. Set out small rubber stamps in the same shape as the dotted outline, along with ink pads in an appropriate color. Let your children stamp the shape on each dot of their outlines. When they have finished, let them add other details with crayons, if desired.

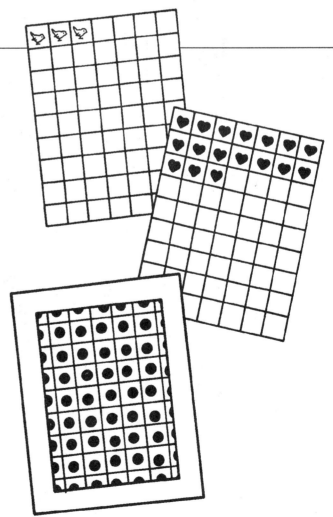

Stamping in Squares

For each child, draw a grid of 1½-inch squares (or squares of any size) on a piece of white paper. Give your children rubber stamps in shapes that will fit inside the squares and set out colored ink pads. Have the children try stamping designs inside the squares on their papers, starting at the top and moving from left to right. When they have finished, frame their papers, if desired, and display them on a wall or a bulletin board.

VARIATION: Give your children pages from an old calendar and let them stamp designs inside the squares.

LANGUAGE

Simple Stories

On a piece of paper, use rubber stamps to print two or three different designs, such as a mouse, a boat, and a flower. At circle time, display the paper and make up a story that includes the stamped pictures. Then let each of your children choose several other rubber stamps and print those designs on a separate piece of paper. Have the children take turns telling stories about their own stamped pictures.

VARIATION: Instead of telling individual stories, let your children work cooperatively on one story.

Silly Story

At group time, put 5 to 10 rubber stamps, in familiar shapes, into a bag. Have your children sit with you around a table and give them ink pads and paper. Let one child begin telling a story by taking a rubber stamp from the bag, stamping the design on paper, and making up a sentence about it. Write down the sentence as the child speaks. Have the other children take turns continuing the story by following the same procedure. When all the stamps have been used, read the story back while the children hold up their stamped pictures. (Note that the story may or may not make sense.)

Concept Stamping

Working with two or three of your children at a time, use rubber stamps to reinforce various concepts. For example, to review *in* and *under*, have the children each draw a picture of a tree on a separate piece of paper. Set out apple stamps and red ink pads. Say, "Three red apples were in the tree," and ask the children to stamp apples on their tree pictures to illustrate your sentence. Continue by saying, "Four red apples were under the tree," and have the children again illustrate your sentence with the apple stamps. Following are other possible concept sentences for your children to illustrate.

- The birds flew *over* the telephone wire, then *under* it.

- Five orange pumpkins were sitting *on* a fence.

- The sun was *up* in the sky, and the flowers were *down* in the garden.

- Some eggs were *inside* the basket, and some eggs were *outside* the basket.

The 🐰 lived in the forest. She was a very happy 🐰. The 🐰 liked flowers. There were lots of flowers in the forest for the 🐰 to find. The 🐰 brought the pretty flowers home to her mother.

Rubber Stamp Stories

Make up a story of several sentences about an animal or other familiar character. Write the story on a large piece of paper. Whenever the character's name appears in the story, use a rubber stamp to make a print of the character instead of writing out its name. As you read the story aloud, pause at each stamped print and let your children "read" the pictured word.

VARIATION: Write your story on paper, leaving a blank square each time the character's name appears. Make copies of the story for your children and let them stamp the character's picture in each square on their papers. Read the story with the children and encourage them to read it with their families when they take their copies home.

Rubber Stamp Books

Make a blank book for each of your children by stapling several pieces of white paper together with a construction-paper cover. Write "My Stamp Book" and the child's name on the front. Set out an assortment of rubber stamps and different-colored ink pads. Let the children decorate their books by stamping different designs on each of the pages. When they have finished, have them "read" their books to you.

Single Character Books

Make a blank book for each of your children. On each page, use a rubber stamp to make an identical print of a character such as a clown or a bear. Have the children use crayons or felt-tip markers to draw pictures on their book pages that incorporate the printed character. As they "read" their books to you, write their words on their book pages, if desired.

Folktale Storybook

Choose a familiar folktale such as "The Three Bears" or "The Three Little Pigs." Make a blank book and write the tale on the pages, using as few words as possible. Set out colored ink pads and rubber stamps in the shapes of the folktale characters (three sizes of bears, three different pigs, etc.). As you read the story to your children, let them stamp illustrations on the pages. Add a cover, let the children decorate it, then place the book in your book corner.

Color Storybooks

For each of your children, staple pieces of white paper together with a construction-paper cover to make a blank book. Write "My Color Storybook" and the child's name on the cover. Use colored felt-tip markers to write a different color name at the bottom of each page. Set out ink pads in matching colors and an assortment of rubber stamps. Have your children stamp red designs on their red pages, blue designs on their blue pages, and so on. When they have finished, encourage them to "read" their books to you.

Group Rubber Stamp Book

Give each of your children a 4-by-6-inch index card. Set out a variety of rubber stamps and different-colored ink pads. Let each child choose a stamp and use it to print a design on his or her card. Ask the child to tell one sentence about the design. As he or she does so, write the sentence on the child's card and add the child's name. Staple all the cards together with a decorative cover to make a group book for the children to "read" to one another.

Rubber Stamp Finger Puppets

For easy finger puppets, use small rubber stamps to print appropriate figures on your children's fingertips. For example, print a kitten on three of each child's fingers before telling the story of the three little kittens. Let your children use their finger puppets to act out the story.

VARIATION: To make hand puppets, use large rubber stamps to print pictures on your children's palms.

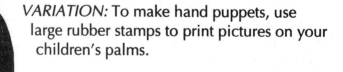

Tongue Depressor Puppets

Print mini-rubber stamp designs on the ends of tongue depressors to make puppets. Have your children manipulate the puppets as you tell stories. Or let the children choose rubber stamps and make their own puppets for acting out original stories.

Stick Puppets

Choose large rubber stamps in desired shapes. Make prints of the shapes on posterboard, cut them out and attach them to the tops of craft sticks. Let your children use the puppets to dramatize the action at storytime.

I Know This Letter

Title pieces of light-colored construction paper or large index cards "I Know This Letter." Keep the papers with a set of alphabet rubber stamps. Whenever a child learns a new letter of the alphabet, give him or her one of the papers and a stamp in the form of that letter. Let the child ink the stamp and press it all over the paper to make prints.

Stamping Letter Shapes

For each of your children, cut a large alphabet letter shape out of light-colored construction paper or posterboard. Set out different-colored ink pads and alphabet rubber stamps. Have your children find letter stamps that match their cutout letters. Then let them cover their letter cutouts with matching letter prints in various colors.

Stamping Paper Shapes

Whenever your children learn a new alphabet letter, cut out construction-paper shapes of something with a name that begins with that letter. Then let the children use alphabet rubber stamps to print that letter all over the cutout shapes. For example, to review the letter *F*, have the children stamp *F*'s on paper fish shapes. Let the children take the shapes home to use for letter review.

Illustrating Letters

When you introduce a new alphabet letter, write that letter on a separate large index card for each of your children. Set out different-colored ink pads and rubber stamps in the shapes of things with names that begin with that letter. For example, set out a clown stamp, a cat stamp, and a candy cane stamp for the letter *C*. Let the children decorate their cards with the rubber stamp pictures. If desired, save each child's cards and staple them together to make an alphabet book.

Alphabet Hunt

Place a piece of butcher paper on the floor. Set out alphabet rubber stamps and ink pads. Let your children make prints of the letters all over the butcher paper. Give them each a different-colored crayon or felt-tip marker. Call out a letter such as *H.* Let the children search for *H's* on the butcher paper and circle them wherever they find them. Continue until all the letters have been circled.

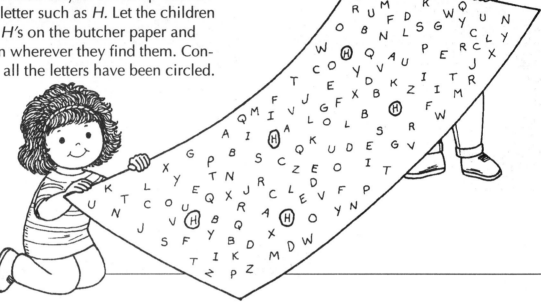

Letter Corrals

For each of your children, divide a piece of paper into fourths to make four "corrals." Use a felt-tip marker to label each corral with a different alphabet letter. Give each child the four alphabet rubber stamps that match the letters on his or her paper. Set out ink pads. Have the children identify the letters in the corrals on their papers and fill each one with matching stamped-on letters.

Stamping Names

Invite one of your children at a time to sit with you at a table. Print the child's name at the top of a piece of light-colored construction paper. Give the child an ink pad and the alphabet rubber stamps that make up the child's name. Ask the child to find the stamp that matches the first letter in his or her name and print that letter under the one on the paper. Have the child continue in the same manner until the entire name has been spelled out. If desired, let the child print his or her name again on the paper, using a different-colored ink pad.

EXTENSION: Let your children spell out the names of friends or family members.

Alphabet Sequencing

Print the letters of the alphabet in sequence on a long piece of paper. Give your children an ink pad and a set of alphabet rubber stamps. Let them find each letter stamp in order, starting with *A,* and print out a copy of the alphabet under the written letters on the paper.

LEARNING GAMES

Color Match

Use rubber stamps and red and blue ink pads to print designs at random on a piece of butcher paper. (Or use any two colors of ink pads.) Place the paper on a low table or on the floor and set out red and blue crayons. Then let your children work together to circle all the red designs on the paper with red crayons and all the blue designs with blue crayons. When the children are ready for a more challenging activity, give them a paper with designs stamped in more than two colors.

VARIATION: Instead of circling the stamped-on designs, have your children connect them with the matching-colored crayons.

Picture Match

Select 10 index cards and divide them into five pairs. Use rubber stamps in the shapes of animals, toys, etc., to print a different picture on each pair of cards. Mix up the cards and place them in a pile. Then let your children take turns finding the cards with matching stamped-on pictures.

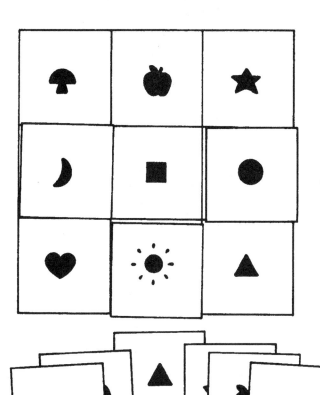

Rubber Stamp Lotto

Make a game board by dividing a 9-inch square of posterboard into nine equal sections. Gather nine small rubber stamps and an ink pad. Use a different stamp to print a design inside each of the sections on the game board. Stamp nine matching designs on another 9-inch posterboard square that has been divided into nine sections. Cut out the sections to make game cards. To play, have your children place the game cards on top of the matching designs on the game board.

VARIATION: Use index cards divided into six sections each to make take-home lotto games. Put the pieces of each game into separate envelopes.

Rubber Stamp Dominoes

Trim 10 index cards to measure 2 ½ by 5 inches each. Select five different rubber stamps. Draw a line across the middle of each card and stamp a different design on each half. (Print four designs with each of the five rubber stamps.) Let your children take turns laying out the cards so that the matching halves are touching, either vertically or horizontally.

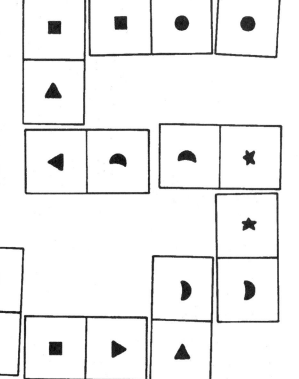

Rubber Stamp Concentration

Divide eight small index cards into pairs. Using four different rubber stamps, print a different design on each pair of cards. To play, mix up the cards and spread them out face down on the floor or a table. Let one child begin by turning up two cards. If the designs match, let the child keep the cards. If the designs do not match, have the child replace both cards face down exactly where they were before. Continue the game until all the cards have been matched.

VARIATION: Instead of using four different rubber stamps, make prints with one stamp in four different colors. Or stamp one design more than once on the pairs of cards to make new, composite designs.

Classifying Colors

For each of your children, divide a piece of white construction paper in half. Label the halves "Yellow" and "Green," using yellow and green crayons. Set out yellow and green ink pads and a variety of rubber stamps. Let your children choose the stamps they wish and use them to print yellow designs on the yellow halves of their papers and green designs on the green halves. Increase the number of colors for a more challenging activity.

Sorting Cards

Select nine small index cards. Divide the cards into sets of three. Use rubber stamps to print pictures of foods on one set, animals on another set, and toys on the third set. (Or use any three categories of picture stamps.) Print the pictures using three different-colored ink pads. Mix up the cards and give them to your children. Have them sort the cards by category or by color.

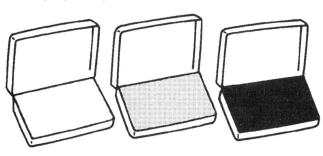

Odd Picture Out

Select four small index cards. On three of the cards, use rubber stamps to print pictures of things that are alike in some way, such as a dog, a pig, and a fish. On the fourth card, print a picture of something that is unlike the other three, such as a car. Follow the same procedure to make other sets of four cards each. To play, spread out a set of cards on a table or on the floor. Invite a child to examine the pictures, tell you which one doesn't belong, and explain why. Continue in the same manner with the other sets of cards.

Creating Patterns

Cut white construction paper into 2-inch-wide strips and give them to your children. Set out different-colored ink pads and give each child two rubber stamps. Let the children experiment, using their stamps to print design patterns or color patterns on their paper strips.

VARIATION: Show your children how to create patterns with one stamp by turning it sideways and upside down.

Pattern Strips

On strips of white posterboard, use a variety of rubber stamps and different-colored ink pads to create patterns. For example, one strip might contain a repeated pattern of a red circle, a blue square, and a yellow triangle. Cover the strips with clear self-stick paper for durability. Set out the rubber stamps and ink pads that were used to make the patterns on the posterboard strips. Let your children copy the patterns on strips of white construction paper.

Copy Cat

Using an assortment of rubber stamps, print a simple pattern across the top of a sheet of construction paper. Give the stamps, the pattern sheet, and an ink pad to one of your children and let him or her duplicate the pattern below the original. Stamp additional patterns on the paper for the child to copy, if desired.

Fill in the Blanks

Use two rubber stamps to print several lines of an "A-B-A-B-A" pattern on a piece of construction paper. Each time you repeat the pattern, leave out the first, middle, or last picture and draw in a blank line. Give the paper to one of your children, along with an ink pad and the two rubber stamps. Let the child complete the patterns by stamping the appropriate designs in the blanks.

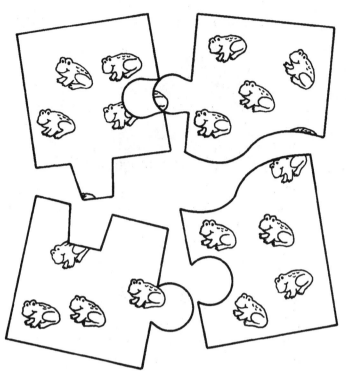

Rubber Stamp Puzzles

Cut a square out of light-colored posterboard. Ink a rubber stamp and use it to print designs all over the square. Then cut the square into several pieces to make a puzzle. Mix up the pieces, give them to your children, and let them take turns putting the puzzle together. Using different rubber stamps, make several additional puzzles. Store the pieces of each one in a separate resealable plastic bag.

Sequence Cards

Make a clear print on paper with a favorite rubber stamp. Use a copy machine that has an enlarger to make copies of the print in several larger sizes. Cut out the different-size prints, glue them on separate index cards, and let your children take turns arranging them from smallest to largest or largest to smallest.

VARIATION: Make a set of Sequence Cards using different-size rubber stamps in the shape of the same object; for example, a small star, a medium-sized star, and a large star.

Hidden Picture Game

Cover a piece of light-colored construction paper with prints made from an assortment of rubber stamps. Choose an additional rubber stamp, such as one in the shape of a kitten. Somewhere among the prints on the paper, stamp one kitten print. Give the paper to your children and ask them to "Find Kitty."

EXTENSION: Let your children make their own Hidden Picture Games to share with one another.

Rubber Stamp Tic-Tac-Toe

Invite two of your children at a time to sit with you at a table. Draw a tic-tac-toe grid on a piece of paper. Give each child a different rubber stamp and set out an ink pad. Also set out game cards that contain different colors, shapes, numerals, etc. Let the children take turns selecting a card and naming the color, shape, etc., on it. For each correct answer, have a child stamp a design in the tic-tac-toe grid. Continue until the grid is filled or until one child completes a straight line of identical stamped-on designs.

Stamping Addresses

Cut pieces of white construction paper into envelope-size rectangles. Show your children where an address is printed on the front of an envelope. Then give each child some of the construction-paper "envelopes," an old address stamp, and an ink pad. Let the children use the stamps to address their envelopes.

VARIATION: Let older children also stamp on return addresses.

Shape Hunt

On index cards, stamp shapes such as circles, squares, triangles, and rectangles. (To make your own shape stamps, see the suggestions on pages 56–61.) Hand out the cards. Then let your children walk around the room and try to find objects that are the same shapes as those stamped on their cards. When everyone has found an appropriate object, have the children exchange cards and start the Shape Hunt again.

Treasure Hunt

In an appropriate place in your room, hide a "treasure" such as cutout paper shapes or small boxes of raisins. Set out clue cards that will lead your children to the hidden treasure. Make the cards by using rubber stamps to print pictures of objects in your room (a wagon, a toy clown, etc.). Give the first card to your children and have them find the object pictured on the card. On that first object, have them find the stamped clue card for the second object they need to find, and so on, until they finally reach the treasure.

Stamp the Tail on the Bunny

Attach a piece of butcher paper to a wall at the children's eye level. In the middle of the paper, draw a back view of a bunny. Have on hand a different-shaped rubber stamp or a different-colored ink pad for each child. One at a time, have each child close his or her eyes. Then guide the child up to the paper and have him or her stamp on a design for the bunny's tail. When everyone has had a turn, check the paper to see who was closest to getting the bunny's tail in the right place.

MATH

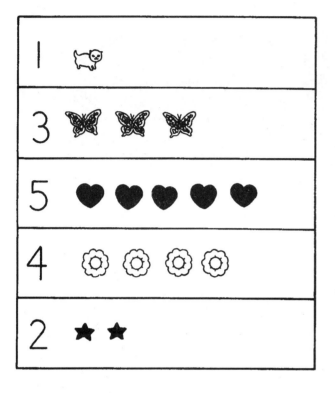

Number Match

For each of your children, draw lines across a separate piece of white construction paper to make five rows. Randomly number the rows from 1 to 5 down the left-hand side. Set out ink pads and five different rubber stamps. Have your children identify the numerals at the beginning of the rows on their papers and stamp corresponding numbers of designs inside the rows (one kitten, four flowers, three butterflies, etc.).

VARIATION: For younger children, number the rows with sets of dots instead of numerals.

How Many Spiders?

Give each of your children a piece of paper with a spider web drawn on it. Add a numeral such as 3. Set out a spider stamp and an ink pad. Let the children take turns stamping three spiders on their spider web pictures.

VARIATION: Instead of stamping spiders on a web, have your children stamp fish inside a fishbowl, bugs on a leaf, apples in a tree, etc.

Grouping Designs

Give each of your children a piece of light-colored construction paper. Set out rubber stamps and ink pads. Let the children stamp designs all over their papers. Then have them group the designs into two's, three's, or four's by drawing circles around the designs with crayons or felt-tip markers.

Addition Stamps

Use rubber stamp designs to illustrate simple addition problems. For example, on an index card, write "2 + 2 = 4." Then, next to each numeral, use a rubber stamp to print corresponding numbers of an identical design. Follow the same procedure to make other addition cards. Let your children use the cards for counting practice.

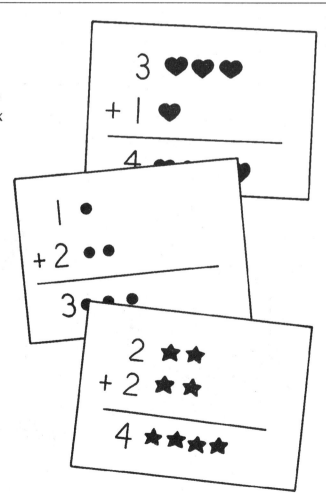

Shapes for Counting

From light-colored construction paper, cut out five seasonal shapes such as hearts (or tear pages from a heart-shaped note pad). Use a felt-tip marker to number the shapes from 1 to 5. Cover the shapes with clear self-stick paper. Set out a small rubber stamp in the shape of a heart and a dark-colored ink pad. Let your children take turns identifying the numerals on the hearts and stamping on corresponding numbers of heart prints. As each child finishes, wipe the ink off the shapes with a damp paper towel.

VARIATION: Draw outlines of seasonal shapes on paper, number them, and have your children fill in the outlines with corresponding numbers of stamped-on matching-shaped prints.

Number Cards

Select 10 index cards and divide them into five pairs. Use a rubber stamp with one color of ink to make one print on one pair of cards, two prints on another pair, three prints on a third pair, and so on. When the ink has dried, mix up the cards and place them in a pile. Let your children take turns finding the matching pairs.

Counting-Card Packs

For each of your children, number five index cards from 1 to 5. Set out ink pads and small rubber stamps. Let your children stamp corresponding numbers of prints on their numbered cards. Give the children envelopes or resealable plastic bags for storing their individual card packs. Encourage them to exchange packs with friends and count one anothers' designs.

VARIATION: For younger children, number the cards with numerals and sets of dots.

Simple Counting Books

Make a blank book for each of your children by stapling 10 pieces of white paper together with a construction-paper cover. Write "My Counting Book" and the child's name on the front. Use a crayon or a felt-tip marker to number the pages of each book from 1 to 10. Set out an assortment of rubber stamps and different-colored ink pads. Then have the children identify the numerals on their book pages and stamp on corresponding numbers of designs.

VARIATION: For younger children, number the book pages with numerals and sets of dots.

Barn Animals Counting Book

Cut a large barn shape out of red posterboard and add details with a felt-tip marker. Cut and fold back the doors. Mount the barn shape on a piece of cardboard. Make a blank book of 10 pages to fit inside the open barn doors and attach the book to the cardboard. Number the pages from 1 to 10. Then use small rubber stamps in the shapes of farm animals to make corresponding numbers of prints on each page (one cow, two sheep, three pigs, etc.). Close the barn doors and give the book to your children. Let them take turns opening the doors, counting the animals on each page, and telling how many animals are in the barn.

Counting By Two's

Make a blank book of five pages. Select a rubber stamp in the shape of a bear face (or any kind of face). Stamp one face on the first page of the book and write "1 bear, 2 eyes" beneath the picture. On the second page, stamp two faces and write "2 bears, 4 eyes" on the page. Continue in the same manner until all five pages have been filled. Add a construction paper cover. Then give the book to your children to use for practicing counting by two's.

VARIATION: Help each child make a book of his or her own. Include as many pages in each book as desired.

Counting Storybook

Make a blank book of 10 white pages and attach a colorful paper cover. Choose a theme such as the circus. With a felt-tip marker, number the book pages from 1 to 10. Then use rubber stamps in the shapes of circus characters to stamp on corresponding numbers of pictures. Let your children make up a story about the numbered circus characters for you to write on the book pages. Let them also add details to the pages with crayons or felt-tip markers to further illustrate their story. Decide on a title with the children and write it on the book cover. Place the book in your book corner for the children to "read" to one another.

Rubber Stamp Money

Purchase rubber stamps in the shapes of different coins (available at school supply stores). Let your children use the stamps to print coin designs on pieces of paper. Then give them real coins to match with their coin prints.

EXTENSION: Help your children cut out their coin prints. Let them use the paper coins as money when playing store.

SCIENCE

Identifying Feelings

Collect rubber stamps in the shapes of faces that have various expressions. Set out the stamps, along with an ink pad. Have one of your children at a time sit with you and give him or her a piece of light-colored construction paper. Ask the child to stamp on a picture of a happy face, a sad face, an angry face, and so on.

VARIATION: Make prints of the face stamps on small index cards. Give the cards to your children and ask them to tell how the character on each card is feeling.

Animal Tracks

Make stamps in the shapes of different animal feet, such as bear paws, duck feet, and horse hooves. (See pages 56–61 for homemade stamp ideas.) Set out large pieces of white construction paper and ink pads. Let your children use the stamps to make animal-track prints on their papers. Discuss how the tracks are alike and how they are different.

VARIATION: Place a piece of white butcher paper on the floor. Let your children stamp on long lines of tracks like those made by walking or running animals.

Stamp and Sniff

Make stamping a sensory experience by providing your children with a variety of scented ink pads. Set out rubber stamps and light-colored paper. Let the children stamp designs on their papers and sniff them. Can they identify the different scents? Encourage the children to share their favorite scented designs with one another.

Nature Walk Graph

Before going on a nature walk, prepare a simple graph by drawing a grid on a large piece of paper. In the left-hand squares of the grid, write category names such as "Birds," "Bugs," "Flowers," and "Animals." When you go on your walk, take along the graph, a rubber stamp for each category, and an ink pad. Whenever the children spot a nature item listed on your graph, stamp a design in one of the squares in the appropriate row. When you return from your walk, use the graph for discussing the nature items you saw.

MUSIC

The Stamping Song

Sing the song below after your children have made pictures with rubber stamps. Each time you sing, substitute the name of one of your children for *Ashley.*

Sung to: "Old MacDonald Had a Farm"

Our friend Ashley has some paper,
E-I-E-I-O.
And on this paper she stamped some prints.
E-I-E-I-O.
With a stamp, stamp here,
    (Make stamping motions with fist.)
And a stamp, stamp there,
Here a stamp, there a stamp,
Everywhere a stamp, stamp.
Our friend Ashley made a picture!
E-I-E-I-O.

Angela Hannaford

Stamp Your Card

Give each of your children an index card, a rubber stamp, and an ink pad. Let the children stamp designs on their cards as you sing the song below. Then have them count and tell the number of prints they have made.

Sung to: "Row, Row, Row Your Boat"

Stamp, stamp, stamp your card,
Stamp it all around.
Now count the stamps that you have made.
How many have you found?

Ellen Bedford

Sing and Stamp

Give your children paper, rubber stamps, and ink pads. Then sing the song below, each time substituting a desired number for *seven* and one of the children's names for *Joseph*. At the end of the song, help the children count the number of prints on their papers.

Sung to: "Mary Had a Little Lamb"

Please pick up your rubber stamp,
Rubber stamp, rubber stamp.
Please pick up your rubber stamp,
We're going to have some fun.

Stamp your paper seven times,
Seven times, seven times.
Stamp your paper seven times,
Stamp until you're done.

Joseph stamped on seven stamps,
Seven stamps, seven stamps.
Joseph stamped on seven stamps,
Now let's count each one.

Jamie Bedford

Ten Little Rubber Stamps

Give each of your children a small rubber stamp, an ink pad, and a piece of paper with the numerals 1 to 10 written on it in sequence. Then sing the song below and have the children stamp on top of each numeral at the appropriate time.

Sung to: "Ten Little Indians"

One little, two little,
Three little rubber stamps,
Four little, five little,
Six little rubber stamps,
Seven little, eight little,
Nine little rubber stamps,
Ten little rubber stamps.

Kathy McCullough

TEACHING MATERIALS

Hand Stamps

• When your children arrive each morning, stamp the backs of their right hands with a seasonal rubber stamp as you greet them at the door. This will help them learn to distinguish between their right and left hands.

• For an award or a prize, use a special rubber stamp to print a design on a child's hand.

• Instead of making "tickets" for a special activity, stamp your children's hands with an appropriate rubber stamp.

• Before going on a field trip, stamp the hands of the children and the adult in each group with an identical rubber stamp. Your children will find it easy to remember which group they belong to and which adult is their leader.

Calendar Pieces

Select a pad of self-stick removable notes that will fit inside the spaces on your wall calendar. At the beginning of September, choose a seasonal rubber stamp such as a leaf stamp. Use the stamp to print a leaf in autumn colors on each of 30 self-stick notes. Number the papers from 1 to 30. Then attach the papers to your wall calendar. Follow the same procedure using a different seasonal stamp at the beginning of each month.

Attendance Chart

On a large piece of construction paper or posterboard, draw the outline of a chart like the one in the illustration. Write your children's names in the spaces down the left-hand side of the chart. In the spaces at the top of the chart, write the names of the days of the week, from Monday to Friday. Title the chart "Our Attendance." When your children arrive in the morning, have a rubber stamp and an ink pad available. Let each child use the stamp to print a design in the proper space after his or her name.

VARIATION: Use the same basic outline to make any other kind of chart. For example, when you are teaching a nutrition unit, make a breakfast chart. Each day, let your children stamp on a design after telling what they ate for breakfast that morning.

Our Attendance	M	T	W	Th	F
Becca	♥	🐦			
Nick	♥	🐦			
Tori	♥				
Ben	♥	🐦			
Nichelle	♥	🐦			
Jessie					
Travis	♥	🐦			
Jodi	♥				
Andrew		🐦			

Parent Communications

Use rubber stamps to decorate special announcements or bulletins that you send home to parents. Choose stamps that correlate with the theme of announcements; for example, print the design of a clock face on an announcement about a time change. The stamped designs will help catch parents' attention and assure that your announcements are read.

Clip Art

Use a rubber stamp and a black ink pad to print seasonal designs, such as Halloween pumpkins, Hanukkah menorahs, or winter snowmen, on white paper. Make several copies of the designs on a copy machine. File the designs away to use as clip art for decorating your parent newsletters.

Stamped Stickers

Make your own stickers to use for awards, decorations, or stamp albums. Cut blank self-stick address labels or plain self-stick paper into desired shapes. Then use a rubber stamp and a bright-colored ink pad to print a design on each shape. Or try stamping designs with small rubber stamps on colored self-stick circles or rectangles.

VARIATION: To make a sheet of stickers, brush a mixture of two parts white glue to one part white vinegar all over a piece of paper. Allow the paper to dry overnight, turn it over, and stamp on colored designs. Cut out the designs to make lick-and-stick stickers.

Outdated Office Stamps

To add to your collection of rubber stamps, ask banks, stores, and other businesses to donate old or outdated office stamps. The stamps can be used for art or writing projects or for post-office play. To clean the stamps, scrub them with an old toothbrush under hot running water.

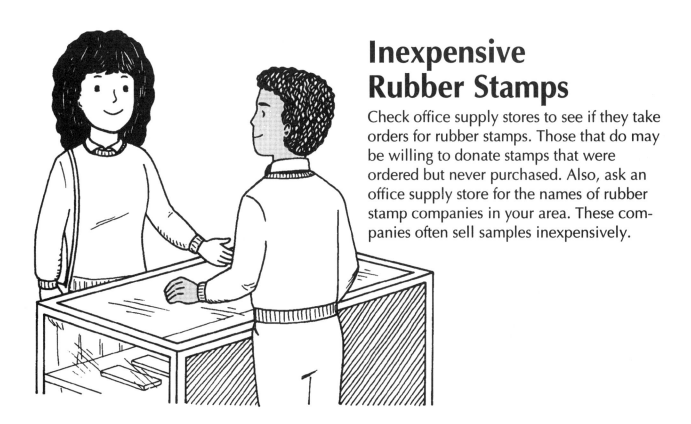

Inexpensive Rubber Stamps

Check office supply stores to see if they take orders for rubber stamps. Those that do may be willing to donate stamps that were ordered but never purchased. Also, ask an office supply store for the names of rubber stamp companies in your area. These companies often sell samples inexpensively.

HOMEMADE STAMPS

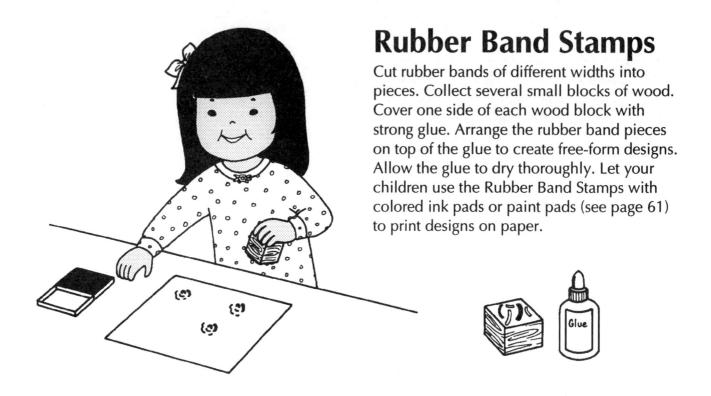

Rubber Band Stamps

Cut rubber bands of different widths into pieces. Collect several small blocks of wood. Cover one side of each wood block with strong glue. Arrange the rubber band pieces on top of the glue to create free-form designs. Allow the glue to dry thoroughly. Let your children use the Rubber Band Stamps with colored ink pads or paint pads (see page 61) to print designs on paper.

Inner-Tube Stamps

Trace the outlines of seasonal or topical shapes on flat pieces of a rubber inner tube. Cut out the shapes with scissors. Then use strong glue to attach the shapes to the sides of small wood blocks. Allow the glue to dry for 24 hours. Let your children use the rubber stamps with ink pads or paint pads (see page 61) to make prints.

Sheet-Rubber Stamps

Purchase a piece of sheet rubber, 3/16-inch to 3/4-inch thick (check the Yellow Pages of your telephone directory to find places where rubber products are sold). Use sharp scissors to cut simple shapes out of the sheet rubber. Then attach the shapes to small blocks of wood, using strong glue. Allow 24 hours for the glue to dry. Set out ink pads or paint pads (see page 61) for your children to use with the Sheet-Rubber Stamps.

Shoe Insole Stamps

Purchase shoe insoles (available at drugstores). Cut seasonal or topical shapes out of the insoles with scissors. Then glue the shapes on the sides of small wood blocks to make stamps. Let your children use the stamps with colored ink pads to make prints on paper.

HINT: Use this method to make stamps from designs that your children create.

Pink Eraser Stamps

Select large, flat pink erasers (available where school supplies are sold). To make each stamp, first draw a seasonal or topical design on one side of an eraser. With a craft knife, cut around the shape to a depth of about ¼ inch. Then cut the eraser away from the outside edges of the shape to create a raised, cutout design. Let your children use the eraser stamps with ink pads or paint pads (see page 61) to make prints.

Gum Eraser Stamps

Purchase large, square gum erasers at an office supply store. Use a craft knife to carve a design into one side of each eraser. Let your children press the carved sides of the erasers on ink pads and then on paper to make prints.

VARIATION: To carve raised designs on the erasers, follow the directions for making Pink Eraser Stamps (above).

Rolling Pin Stamper

For this activity, you will need a rolling pin, vinyl flooring, sturdy shears, and strong glue. You will also need an oven set at 150°F. Soften the flooring for about 3-5 minutes on a baking sheet in the oven. Use the shears to cut seasonal or topical shapes out of the flooring. Place the shapes back on the baking sheet and into the oven to make them soft and pliable. Gently bend each shape around the rolling pin and glue it in place with heavy glue. When the glue has dried thoroughly, give the Rolling Pin Stamper to your children. Let them roll it in a pan containing a small amount of tempera paint and then on butcher paper to make prints.

HINT: Use your Rolling Pin Stamper to make wrapping paper or wallpaper.

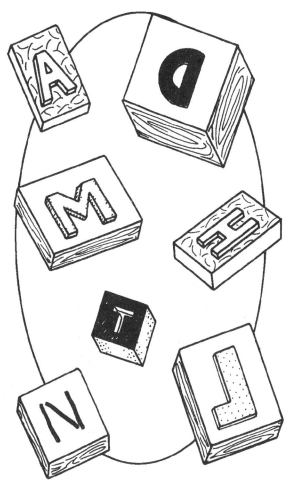

Alphabet Letter Stamps

Make your own letter stamps using one or more of the methods described on pages 56–58. Trace the letter shapes using stencils or other guides. Before gluing the letter shapes onto wood blocks or carving them out of erasers, be sure to reverse them so that they will print correctly. Let your children use the stamps with ink pads or paint pads (see page 61) to print letters or short words.

VARIATION: Instead of individual letter stamps, make simple word stamps or stamps that spell out your children's names. Be sure to reverse the letters and arrange them from right to left as you are making the stamps.

Stamp Handles

Besides using small blocks of wood for your homemade stamp handles, try gluing cutout shapes to objects such as the ones below.

- thread spools
- corks
- jar lids
- small boxes
- film canisters

More Stamping Materials

Try gluing any of the items below onto wood blocks or other handles to make stamps.

- buttons
- pasta wheels
- pasta alphabet letters
- shapes cut from cardboard
- shapes cut from plastic foam
- flat erasers in animal or other shapes

Disposable Ink Pads

Make inked stamp pads for your children to use. For each pad, cut a small square out of felt and place it in a plastic-foam food tray. Select a colored stamp-pad inker (available where rubber stamps are sold). Then roll ink onto the felt squares until they are slightly damp. Have the children press rubber stamps on the felt squares, then on pieces of paper to make prints. At the end of the activity, just throw the ink pads away.

Paint Stamp Pads

Let your children try printing with rubber stamps and tempera paint. Following are suggestions for two kinds of paint pads you can make.

Paper Towel Pad—Place folded paper towels in a shallow container and pour on a small amount of tempera paint. Have your children press rubber stamps on the towels, then on paper to make prints.

Sponge Stamp Pad—Cut a flat sponge to fit inside a travel soap-bar case with a lid (available at large drugstores). Pour a small amount of tempera paint on the sponge. Let your children press rubber stamps on the sponge, then on paper. Keep the lid on the case when not in use to prevent the paint from drying out.

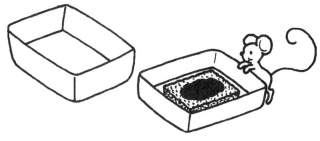

PIGGYBACK® SONG SERIES
Repetition and rhyme

New songs to the tunes of child-hood favorites. No music to read.

Piggyback® Songs
A seasonal collection of more than 100 original songs on 64 pages.
WPH 0201 .... $7.95

More Piggyback® Songs
More seasonal songs—180 in all—in this collection, which spans 96 pages.
WPH 0202 .... $8.95

Piggyback® Songs to Sign
Four new signing phrases to use each month along with new Piggyback songs.
WPH 0209 .... $8.95

Holiday Piggyback® Songs
More than 250 original songs for 15 holidays and other celebrations.
WPH 0206 .... $8.95

Piggyback® Songs for School
Delightful songs to use throughout the school day. Favorites in this 96-page book include songs for getting acquainted, transitions, storytime, movement, and cleanup time.
WPH 0208 .... $8.95

Animal Piggyback® Songs
More than 200 songs about farm, zoo, and sea animals.
WPH 0207 .... $8.95

Piggyback® Songs for Infants and Toddlers
This special collection of more than 170 songs is just right for infants and toddlers. Also appropriate for children 3 to 5.
WPH 0203 .... $7.95

1•2•3 SERIES
These books emphasize beginning hands-on activities—creative art, no-lose games, puppets, and more. Designed for children ages 3 to 6.

1•2•3 Art
Open-ended art activities emphasizing the creative process are included in this 160-page book. All 238 activities use inexpensive, readily available materials.
WPH 0401 .... $14.95

1•2•3 Games
Each of the 70 no-lose games in this book are designed to foster creativity and decision making for a variety of ages.
WPH 0402 .... $7.95

1•2•3 Colors
160 pages of activities for "Color Days," including art, learning games, language, science, movement, music, and snacks.
WPH 0403 .... $14.95

NEW! 1•2•3 Science
A collection of fun and wonder-filled activities that gets children excited about science and helps develop early science skills such as predicting and estimating.
WPH 0410 .... $14.95

1•2•3 Rhymes, Songs & Stories
Capture the imaginations of young children with these open-ended rhymes, songs, and stories.
WPH 0408 .... $8.95

1•2•3 Puppets
More than 50 simple puppets to make for working with young children, including Willie Worm, Dancing Spoon, and more.
WPH 0404 .... $7.95

1•2•3 Math
This book has activities galore for experiencing number concepts such as sorting, measuring, time, and ages.
WPH 0409 .... $14.95

1•2•3 Reading & Writing
Meaningful and nonthreatening activities help young children develop *pre-reading* and *pre-writing* skills.
WPH 0407 .... $14.95

1001 SERIES
These books are the ultimate resources for anyone who works with young children.

NEW! 1001 Teaching Tips
Busy teachers on limited budgets need all the help they can get. By combining the best ideas submitted to the *Totline* newsletter, we are able to bring teachers 1001 shortcuts to success! Three major sections include curriculum tips, room tips, and special times tips.
WPH 1502 .... $16.95

NEW! 1001 Rhymes & Fingerplays
This is the ultimate language resource for parents and teachers! Included are rhymes for every day and every occasion! Also included are poems about self, cooperation, and the environment.
WPH 1503 .... $21.95

1001 Teaching Props
These 1001 ideas for using new and recyclable materials make it easy to plan projects, set up discovery centers, and make learning resources. Also includes a handy materials index!
WPH 1501 .... $18.95

SNACK SERIES

A most delicious series of books that provides healthy opportunities for fun and learning.

Super Snacks
This revised edition includes nutritional information for CACFP programs and recipes for treats that contain no sugar, honey, or artificial sweeteners!
WPH 1601 .... $6.95

NEW! Healthy Snacks
More than 100 recipes for healthy alternatives to junk-food snacks! Each recipe is low in fat, sugar, and sodium.
WPH 1602 .... $6.95

NEW! Teaching Snacks
This book promotes the teaching of basic skills and concepts through cooking. Extend learning into snacktime!
WPH 1603 .... $6.95

12/93

THEME-A-SAURUS® SERIES

These books are designed to supply you with handy, instant resources for those moments when you need to expand curiosity into meaningful learning experiences.

Theme-A-Saurus®
Grab instant action with more than 50 themes from Apple to Zebra, and more than 600 activity ideas.
WPH 1001 .... $19.95

Theme-A-Saurus® II
New opportunities for hands-on learning with 60 more theme units that range from Ants to Zippers.
WPH 1002 .... $19.95

Toddler Theme-A-Saurus®
Capture the attention of toddlers with 60 teaching themes that use safe and appropriate materials.
WPH 1003 .... $19.95

Alphabet Theme-A-Saurus®
Giant letter recognition units are filled with hands-on activities that introduce young children to the ABCs.
WPH 1004 .... $19.95

Nursery Rhyme Theme-A-Saurus®
Capture children's enthusiasm with nursery rhymes and related learning activities in this 160-page book.
WPH 1005 .... $14.95

Storytime Theme-A-Saurus®
This book combines 12 storytime favorites with fun and meaningful hands-on activities and songs.
WPH 1006 .... $14.95

CELEBRATION SERIES

Capture children's interest and enthusiasm with these teaching themes based on celebrations for special learning days!

Small World Celebrations
Multicultural
Teach children about other cultures with these multicultural hands-on activities that introduce popular holidays and festivals from around the world.
WPH 0701 .... $14.95

Special Day Celebrations
Nontraditional units
Turn ordinary days into "special days" and get the most out of each learning opportunity. This book offers many suggestions for 50 fun mini-celebrations.
WPH 0702 .... $14.95

Great Big Holiday Celebrations
Traditional units
This is the ultimate learning resource for celebrating all the major holidays. Included are ideas for hands-on learning activities for all kinds of celebrations.
WPH 0704 .... $16.95

EXPLORING SERIES

Environments
Instill the spirit of exploration with these beginning science books that let you take activities as far as your children's interest will go.

NEW! Exploring Sand
Set up a child-directed learning environment with this resource. Contains hands-on activity suggestions for learning with sand and about the desert environment and preserving it.
WPH 1801 .... $8.95

NEW! Exploring Water
This 96-page book is water fun at its best. Offers a full around-the-curriculum unit using water plus an introduction to the ocean environment with an emphasis on preservation.
WPH 1802 .... $8.95

NEW! Exploring Wood
This guide for a child-directed learning environment includes activities for developing early carpentry skills and acquiring knowledge about forests.
WPH 1803 .... $8.95